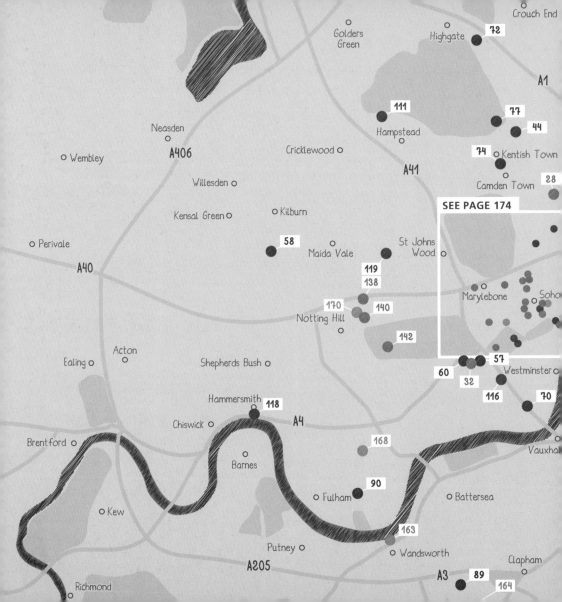

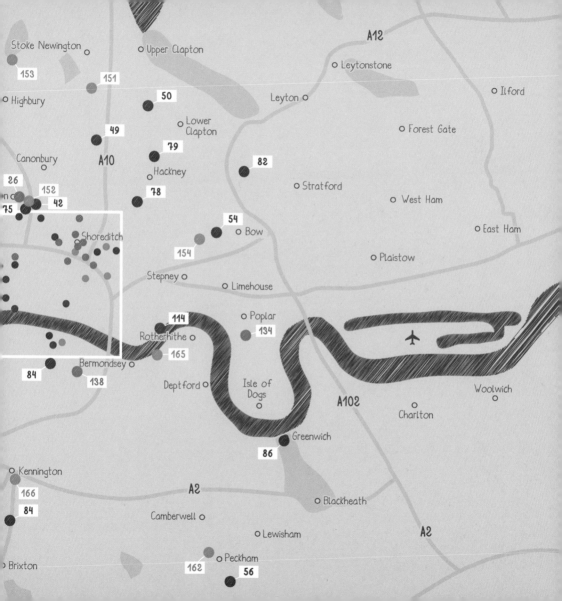

DRINK LONDON

THE 100 BEST BARS AND PUBS

EUAN FERGUSON

PHOTOGRAPHS BY KIM LIGHTBODY

F

FRANCES LINCOLN LIMITED
PUBLISHERS

PIN T GLASS - £4, T-SHIRT - £10

HOODY/SWEATSHIRT - £20

CRAFT BEER WORLD BOOK - £15

PINT - £4, HALF - £2, FLIGHT - £6, PITCH R - £14

GROWLERS

WLER (1.6 PINTS): BOTTLE - £2.50, FILL - £

R (3.2 PINTS): BOTTLE - £5, FILL - £1

B NG YOUR OTTLE BACK FOR A RE-FILL

BREWERY LOCALS GET 10% OFF GROWLERS & TAKE-AWAY

COOKING TONIGHT...

HELLS   WIT   HELLS   INK   WIT   SIERRA   USA   BYRON   UNF
                                          NEVADA   HELLS   PALE   HELLS

ES
XA

CONTENTS

MAP · 2
INTRODUCTION · 8

COCKTAILS ● 10

LEGENDARY LOCALS ● 38

CRAFT BEER, ALE & CIDER ● 62

LIQUID HISTORY ● 92

WINE & SPIRITS SPECIALISTS ● 120

WITH A TWIST ● 144

TICK INDEX · 172
CENTRAL LONDON MAP · 174

INTRODUCTION

What makes a great bar or pub? Personal service, fancy fixtures and furnishings, cutting-edge cocktails? Or a familiar welcome, well-cellared ales, a real fire? Somewhere to set the pulse racing or somewhere quiet to escape to? There's really no straight answer.

With more than 7,000 licensed premises in London, no one's going to go thirsty, but the choice can be bewildering. Given too that they're all spread over an area of 600 square miles, it makes the simple act of going for a drink rather complicated. But here's your guide, no matter what the occasion: a date that needs impressing, a party of pals who need entertaining, an out-of-towner who needs a tour of the city's ancient or eccentric watering holes, or simply an afternoon that needs whiling away in peace and quiet. And there's no 'not bad' or 'it'll do' – from the thousands of contenders in every corner of the capital, these are the 100 best, each one unique, memorable or simply unrivalled at what they do.

Think of this book as a helpful, knowledgeable (and sociable) friend, someone who always knows the perfect setting to answer that age-old question: shall we go for a drink?

COCKTAILS

LONDON COCKTAIL CLUB • 14

EXPERIMENTAL COCKTAIL CLUB • 14

COCKTAIL LOUNGE AT THE

ZETTER TOWNHOUSE • 16

OSKAR'S BAR • 18

MILK & HONEY • 18

COBURG BAR AT THE CONNAUGHT • 20

PUNCH ROOM • 21

BAR AMÉRICAIN • 22

MARK'S BAR • 24

69 COLEBROOKE ROW • 26

GRAIN STORE • 28

HAPPINESS FORGETS • 28

NIGHTJAR • 30

THE BLUE BAR • 32

CALLOOH CALLAY • 34

WHITE LYAN • 34

WORSHIP STREET WHISTLING SHOP • 35

HAWKSMOOR • 36

COCKTAILS

London is the undisputed cocktail capital of the world.
Its stars behind the bar never stand still, continually innovating and challenging perceptions of what it's possible to do with a shelf of spirits, a shaker and a few ice cubes. Places like Worship Street Whistling Shop, 69 Colebrooke Row and Nightjar incorporate all sorts of homemade and high-tech ingredients in their original creations, but it's not all about molecular mixology and the appliance of science. Some say the peak of the bartender's skill is the classic cocktail – Sazeracs, Manhattans, Daquiris – and in London they're made better than anywhere else.
Don't forget either about the many five-star hotel bars in the city.
It's a common misconception that you have to be either rich or a guest (or both) to drink in the likes of the Savoy, the Connaught or the Goring, but for the price of a cocktail anyone can be treated like royalty for an hour or so. It's an experience to be tried at least once.

● LONDON COCKTAIL CLUB

Drink... in a high-spirited saturnalia of cocktail celebration.

Some bars are about exclusivity, refinement, multisensory creations which push the boundaries of mixology. But not London Cocktail Club. It's a place to simply forget the cruel world outside, let your hair down and have a whole load of fun. The decor's loud, the music's loud, the crowd's loud and the cocktails aren't shy either. A comprehensive list covers everything from a Cuba Libre to the more out-there Bacon, Egg & Fries Martini: a real liquid lunch. LCC is a great place to lose an evening.

ESSENTIAL ORDER The pudding-like Rhubarb and Custard Flip comes with a little tub of Ambrosia.
61 Goodge Street, Fitzrovia, W1T 1TL.
☎ *020 7580 1960*
🖳 *www.londoncocktailclub.co.uk*
⊖ *Goodge Street tube. Branches at Shaftesbury Avenue, Shoreditch, Oxford Circus.*

● EXPERIMENTAL COCKTAIL CLUB

Drink... vintage spirits that are probably older than you.

Scents of barbecued duck and aniseed turn the heads of Chinatown tourists, but those in the know head straight to a scuffed and anonymous door at No 13a. It leads into one of the most secretive of London's bars, a dimly lit den of cocktail extravagance. A bit of sweet-talk directed the doorman's way is sometimes required if you've not booked, but a treat awaits once inside – the drinks are among the most distinguished in the city. Further excitement: there's a cabinet of vintage spirits, including 1950s Martell XO and twentieth-century gins. Experimental Cocktail Club is hard to find, hard to get into, even harder to leave.

ESSENTIAL ORDER A Vintage Purgatory (1951 Old Overholt rye, 1950s Benedictine, 1970s chartreuse).
13a Gerrard Street, Chinatown, W1D 5PS.
🖳 *www.chinatownecc.com*
⊖ *Piccadilly Circus tube.*

● COCKTAIL LOUNGE AT THE ZETTER TOWNHOUSE

Drink… in a curiosity shop of a cocktail bar.

It's that easy to get carried away in here. Like an auction house storeroom magically arranged into a bar, Zetter Townhouse is an endlessly fascinating mishmash of furniture, taxidermy (look for the boxing kangaroo), porcelains, paintings, portraits and assorted *objets d'art*. There are numerous studded sofas to squish into, but sit at the bar to watch the action as the friendly staff create dainty cocktails (the prices are pleasant too). It's overseen by Tony Conigliaro, something of a legend on the London bar scene (see his 69 Colebrooke Row on p26).

ESSENTIAL ORDER The Flintlock illustrates the Zetter's creativity and theatre: gin, gunpowder tea tincture, sugar, dandelion and burdock bitters, and Fernet Branca, served with a bang…

49 St John's Square, Farringdon, EC1V 4JJ.
☎ *020 7324 4545*
🖳 *www.thezettertownhouse.com*
⊖ *Farringdon tube.*

● OSKAR'S BAR

Drink... Michelin-starred cocktails.

Okay, the Michelin star applies to the food at upstairs restaurant Dabbous, not the drinks in this industrial-chic basement bar. But if the inspectors handed out plaudits for cocktails too, the incredible creations here would surely be worthy. They display some of the same Scandinavian influences as young chef Ollie Dabbous's food, and often read more like recipes for dinner rather than drink.

Even if you can't stretch to a meal upstairs (or you didn't book weeks in advance), Oskar's is a winner in itself.

ESSENTIAL ORDER Ask for the Drink With No Name – bourbon, greengage liqueur, lemon, agave, ginger ale and Nils Oscar God Lager from Sweden.

39 Whitfield Street, Fitzrovia, W1T 2SF.
☎ *020 7323 1544* 🖥 *www.dabbous.co.uk*
⊖ *Goodge Street tube.*

● MILK & HONEY

Drink... in the dark.

Visitors here make much of the lack of light in this multifloor Soho cocktail hideaway. It certainly is dim, although far from dingy. When your eyes adjust you'll make out a small but smart bar with Prohibition-era design touches, and nattily dressed barman pouring some of the meanest cocktails in London. They sound unshowy – straightforward lists of spirits with no mention of brands – but they're consistently and precisely made. Note: it's mostly members only, although the rest of us can visit until 11pm (and it's worth it). Without a reservation, though, don't even try.

ESSENTIAL ORDER The list is long, but try a London Calling: gin, sherry, lemon, sugar, bitters.

61 Poland Street, Soho, W1F 7NU.
☎ *020 7065 6800* 🖥 *www.mlkhny.com*
⊖ *Oxford Circus tube.*

● COBURG BAR AT THE CONNAUGHT

Drink... in the city's most charming hotel bar.

The imposing Regency edifice of the Connaught is quite the landmark in this villagey part of Mayfair, and it comes with two world-class bars: there's not much in terms of appeal to separate the Coburg Bar (a subtly modern and warm update of an old room) from the Connaught Bar (sleeker, shimmeringly opulent). The Connaught has a mobile martini trolley, but the Coburg has an incredible cocktail menu, a chronological catalogue of classics. There are also dozens of gins, vodkas and rums, and bottlers'-edition cask whiskies; the champagne list is one of the most outstanding in London. If you've bagged a seat, raise a glass. **ESSENTIAL ORDER** From the 1800s to contemporary creations, every cocktail is flawless. *The Connaught, Carlos Place, Mayfair, W1K 2AL.*
☎ *020 7499 7070*
▣ *www.the-connaught.co.uk*
⊖ *Green Park tube.*

● PUNCH ROOM

Drink... the oldest mixed drinks in the world.

The Lobby Bar in the swanky Edition hotel is a sumptuously appointed Regency wonder with lofty ceilings and a chattering crowd, but through the back is the dark, discreet and clubby Punch Room, a reservations-only room specialising in the ancient drink of choice of pirates and privateers, first brought to the West in the 1600s. Settle into a plush leather armchair and peruse the concise list, which ranges from tropical blends made with coconut and angostura to homegrown versions flavoured with oak moss syrup and tea.

ESSENTIAL ORDER The potent and tangy Oxford Punch, with port, cognac, rum, green tea, lemon sherbet and orange sherbet.

London Edition, 10 Berners Street, Fitzrovia, W1T 3NP.

☎ *020 7781 0000*

⌨ *www.edition-hotels. marriott.com/london*

⊖ *Tottenham Court Road tube.*

● BAR AMÉRICAIN

Drink... in a 1930s bar that puts the Prohibition-era pretenders to shame.
Right next to touristy Piccadilly Circus, the basement of the former Regent Palace Hotel has undergone a few transformations since it opened in 1915; its current incarnation makes it one of the most democratically spectacular cocktail bars in London. The beaux arts decor is indeed beautiful, with repeated airplane motifs and woodblock pillars – it benefitted from the cream of the early twentieth century's art deco design expertise, and makes the most of it today. But anyone can walk in off the street attired however they choose and partake of the truly excellent cocktails.
ESSENTIAL ORDER The classics are consummate, the original creations better. Try something from the 'house cocktails' list.
20 Sherwood Street, Soho, W1F 7ED.
☎ *020 7734 4888*
🖥 *www.brasseriezedel.com/bar-americain*
⊖ *Piccadilly Circus tube.*

● MARK'S BAR

Drink... your way around Britain.

Chef Mark Hix, whose flagship restaurant is on the ground floor, is a proud proponent of cooking with seasonal, British, seldom-seen ingredients. This effortlessly cool and clubby bar in the basement does the same with its cocktails. Redcurrant syrup, Burrow Hill Farm cider, sea buckthorn – even green pea-infused London dry gin and atholl brose (Scottish oatmeal dessert)

appear in the stunning concoctions. There are also Hix's own beers, a great wine list and some first-rate bar snacks (scotched quail's eggs, for instance). All round, one of the most agreeable places to drink in London.

ESSENTIAL ORDER The Hix Fix is a modern classic – Somerset apple eau de vie, morello cherry and sparkling English wine.

66 Brewer Street, Soho, W1F 9UP.

☎ *020 7292 3518* 🖳 *www.marksbar.co.uk*

⊖ *Piccadilly Circus tube.*

● 69 COLEBROOKE ROW

Drink... cocktails made of stone.
Or, to be precise, cocktails made
of distilled clay and flint. The
drink in question, the Terroir, also
involves lichen, and is perhaps
the most attention-grabbing mix
at this diminutive Islington spot.
Who wouldn't be intrigued by the
Avignon too, with cognac, camomile
and smoked frankincense, or the
Woodland Martini, which lists
'woodland bitters (maple, cedar and
sequoia)' among its constituents?
On Thursdays and Fridays, a pianist in
the corner serenades what is probably
too small to be called 'the crowd'; an
unmarked exterior and tie-sporting
staff add to the sense you've arrived
somewhere worth seeking out.
ESSENTIAL ORDER A Prairie
Oyster: 'tomato yolk', horseradish
vodka, sherry, shallots, pepper sauce,
celery salt, micro herbs, served in an
oyster-shaped ceramic.
69 Colebrooke Row, Islington,
N1 8AA.
☎ *07540 528593*
🖥 *www.69colebrookerow.com*
⊖ *Angel tube.*

DEATH IN VENICE

15ML CAMPARI
3 DASHES GRAPEFRUIT BITTERS
TOP WITH PROSSECO

CAMPAR

LAGO DI
GARDA

RIVA TORBOLE

69
COLEBROOKE ROW

● GRAIN STORE

Drink... like the Romans.
Master mixologist Tony Conigliaro (see 69 Colebrooke Row, p26, and Zetter Townhouse, p17) is behind the inventive drinks at this bar and restaurant in a converted King's Cross warehouse; he's avoided the classic cocktail cliches and created something classical instead. 'Greco-Roman wines' include the imperial Rose Vinus Lupus, with dried rose petals, clover honey, verjus (acidic grape juice) and gewurztraminer. Visit on a sunny evening and the fountain-splashed square out the front looks almost Continental.
ESSENTIAL ORDER The savoury cocktails and vinous infusions are ingenious.
1 Stable Street, King's Cross, N1C 4AB.
☎ *020 7324 4466* 🖥 *www.grainstore.com* ● *King's Cross tube.*

● HAPPINESS FORGETS

Drink... in the best bar in N1.
Hoxton has come a long way from when it was *the* coolest area of London: you have to hunt out the great places out these days. And here's one of the greatest, right in the former hipster nucleus of Hoxton Square, down an unmarked stairway, below a restaurant – it's a dark, tiny, unelaborately furnished and ultra-classy operation that always gets everything right. Superior cocktails, ultra-smooth service, happy people: visit once and you'll never forget it.
ESSENTIAL ORDER The Perfect Storm exemplifies the cleverly modified classics on the menu – dark rum, honey, lemon and ginger juice and plum brandy.
8 Hoxton Square, Hoxton, N1 6NU.
🖥 *www.happinessforgets.com* ● *Old Street tube.*

● NIGHTJAR

Drink... through the jazz age.
This is how to ace a trend without jumping on the bandwagon. Nightjar is the closest London has to the sort of place Al Capone might have demanded protection money from in 1920s Chicago. There's live jazz most nights, waistcoated staff, seriously low levels of lighting and a completely unmarked entrance on a grotty bit of east London road. But standards are so high that every night out here is special. Is there a more inventive and appealing-sounding cocktail list in London? A more accommodating welcome? It's doubtful.

ESSENTIAL ORDER The drinks list reaches a peak with the Toronto: bourbon, roasted pecan maple syrup, Fernet Branca and orange blossom candy floss.
129 City Road, Shoreditch, EC1V 1JB.
☎ *020 7253 4101*
🖾 *www.barnightjar.com*
⊖ *Old Street tube.*

● THE BLUE BAR

Drink... in an extremely flattering shade of blue.

David Collins was responsible for the design of many of London's swankiest hotel bars, but this hideaway in the fashionable Berkeley is perhaps his most striking. The listed Edwardian plasterwork has been finished head-to-toe in a fetching lavender, with cornflower seats and a black onyx bar providing eye-catching contrast. Cocktails, especially the painstakingly assembled seasonal editions, are spectacular; take time to look at the spirits list, even just to prove there is such a thing as a £928 shot of whisky (Macallan 55 year old).

ESSENTIAL ORDER The Old Roger is typical: rum, homemade eucalyptus and wormwood cordial, and cherry bitters.

The Berkeley, Wilton Place, Knightsbridge, SW1X 7RL.
☎ *020 7235 6000*
▣ *www.the-berkeley.co.uk*
⊖ *Knightsbridge tube.*

● CALLOOH CALLAY

Drink... behind the looking glass.

The cocktails in this award-winning institution (it is an institution in Shoreditch terms, at least – it opened in 2008) aren't experimental, they aren't molecular, they aren't inspired by the handwritten notes of an 'acclaimed St Louis Prohibition-era bartender'. They are, however, great fun, highly original and eminently drinkable. The front bar is packed nightly: make a booking for the 'secret' room at the back, accessed through a mirrored wardrobe (hence the Lewis Carroll-referencing name).

ESSENTIAL ORDER The marvellous cocktail list changes every six months; whatever you pick is guaranteed to be brilliant.

65 Rivington Street, Shoreditch, EC2A 3AY.
☎ *020 7739 4781* 🖥 *www.calloohcallaybar.com*
⊖ *Old Street tube.*

● WHITE LYAN

Drink... the mad creations of a cocktail visionary.

No ice, no branded spirits, no citrus, sugar or perishables... No exaggeration, this first permanent venture by trailblazing cocktail pro Ryan Chetiyawardana is unlike any other bar. Hours of preparation before each service results in a pre-chilled range of spirits (made especially for Ryan or cut with his own distillations), bitters, atomisations, infusions and other uncategorisable ingredients: beeswax egg, pomegranate paint, lager syrup. It's a small, sparsely decorated space, with an under-the-radar location and a following among cocktail thrillseekers. It's also disarmingly friendly.

ESSENTIAL ORDER A reimagined version of your favourite cocktail. It could change the way you think about drinks.

153 Hoxton Street, Hoxton, N1 6PJ.
☎ *020 3011 1153* 🖳 *www.whitelyan.com*
⊖ *Hoxton Overground.*

● WORSHIP STREET WHISTLING SHOP

Drink... in a Dickensian cocktail laboratory.
'Coriander and black pepper hydrosol', 'raspberry and mustard cordial', 'banana and clove vinegar'... These are not ordinary ingredients to find behind the bar, but WSWS is no ordinary bar. In a corner of this dark and enigmatic basement in a quiet part of Shoreditch there's a high-tech set-up involving a distilling machine, a water bath and a liquid-nitrogen freezer; if science leaves you baffled, you can ignore it safe in the knowledge that it results in some of the most fabulous drinks in London.

ESSENTIAL ORDER The signature drink is the Black Cats, with Tanqueray, vermouth, 'removed cream' (ask for the elaborate explanation) and a radish garnish.

63 Worship Street, Shoreditch, EC2A 2DU.
☎ *020 7247 0015* 🖳 *www.whistlingshop.com*
⊖ *Liverpool Street tube.*

● HAWKSMOOR

Drink... where the steaks are high class and the cocktails rarefied.

Hawksmoor is known for its sensational cuts of best-of-British beef, but downstairs (in what was once a Russian strip club) at its Spitalfields branch is an always-lively bar which serves drinkers as well as diners. It looks timeless, but the fittings are all cleverly salvaged; the wall tiles, for instance, came from a St James's hotel lift shaft.

Cocktails are witty and excellent: five special drinks are chosen monthly by one of Hawksmoor's talented bartenders.

ESSENTIAL ORDER Shaky Pete's Ginger Brew: a modern classic with ginger syrup, lemon, gin and London Pride ale.

157a Commercial Street, Spitalfields, E1 6BJ.
☎ *020 7426 4856* 🖥 *www.thehawksmoor.com*
⊖ *Shoreditch High Street Overground.*
Branches at Air Street, Guildhall, Seven Dials.

LEGENDARY LOCALS

THE QUEEN'S HEAD • 42

THE ISLAND QUEEN • 42

THE PINEAPPLE • 45

THE CHARLES LAMB • 45

THE WENLOCK ARMS • 46

THE RAILWAY TAVERN ALE HOUSE • 48

THE CLAPTON HART • 50

THE CARPENTER'S ARMS • 52

THE LORD TREDEGAR • 54

THE OLD FOUNTAIN • 54

THE IVY HOUSE • 56

THE GRENADIER • 57

PARADISE BY WAY OF KENSAL RISE • 58

THE NAG'S HEAD • 60

LEGENDARY LOCALS

Every Londoner, from Wimbledon to Walthamstow, has a local. And every Londoner thinks their local is the best. In a way, they're right: when it comes to drinking there's a time for excitement and a time for familiarity, and familiarity is what you get in your favourite neighbourhood pub. It's unlikely that everyone knows your name, or that your order's being poured as soon as you're through the door; but maybe a nod of recognition from the landlord, a favourite seat by the fire, a pat for the pub dog and a short walk home at the end of the night is enough. Even if you're not propping up the bar every night (not recommended, of course), it's comforting to know it's there. But some locals are worth a visit even if you don't live nearby. These are places that bring something different to the backstreets and 'villages' of London – a brilliant beer selection, say (the Old Fountain), or a family-friendly spirit (Paradise by Way of Kensal Green), or that indefinable good feeling you get as soon as you enter (all of these following places). Some of them are so good that you might be glancing speculatively in estate agents' windows after you leave, wondering if a good local is reason enough to move house.

onsite microbrewery began operation in 2014. What's more, there's a piano – nothing says 'local' like a singalong.

ESSENTIAL ORDER It's an award-winning cider pub – there's always a couple of artisan varieties on the bar.

66 Acton Street, King's Cross, WC1X 9NB.
☎ *020 7713 5772* 🖥 *www.queensheadlondon.com*
⊖ *King's Cross tube.*

● THE ISLAND QUEEN

Drink... in a Victorian Club Tropicana.
She's quite a looker, this Islington queen. The job was started in the late nineteenth century, when a landlord with a taste for the exotic turned the pub into a colonial fantasy of Caribbean life, with ornate glass, painted mirrors and a carved figurehead of the titular queen herself. Food is served, but the thoughtful drinks selection suggests this is as much a place for liquid as solid refreshment. Locals in this pretty part of town are spoilt for choice when it comes to pubs, and the Island Queen is one of the brightest jewels in the crown.

ESSENTIAL ORDER This classic gin palace has a good few London gins, so have one with tonic and luxuriate in the Raj-era atmosphere.

87 Noel Road, Islington, N1 8HD.
☎ *020 7354 8741*
🖥 *www.theislandqueenislington.co.uk*
⊖ *Angel tube.*

● THE QUEEN'S HEAD

Drink... in 'the best pub in London'
...or so a sign outside states. A claim too far, maybe, but the Queen's Head is a very noble proposition all the same. The streets around the great stations are generally uninspiring in pub terms, which makes this cosy and friendly place near King's Cross stand out even more. Preserving many of its original Victorian features, it's run by a genuine beer and cider devotee who changes the casks and kegs on offer regularly, and his

● THE PINEAPPLE

Drink… in a backstreet boozer you'll want to come back to again and again.

In an area embarrassingly rich with good pubs, the Pineapple stands head-and-shoulders higher, and not just for its wonderful throwback name (imagine how exotic the spiky fruit must have seemed to Victorians used to domestic damsons and plain old plums). Thanks to motivated locals it survived an attempt in the early 2000s to develop it into apartments. It's an easygoing place that's at once convivial, cosy or comforting, suiting drinkers sociable and solitary alike; Kentish Towners are kept busy here with live comedy, a fiendish quiz, seasonal singalongs and a cheese-celebration night called… Cheese Night.

ESSENTIAL ORDER There's usually a real ale from Tottenham's Redemption to tuck in to.

51 Leverton Street, Kentish Town, NW5 2NX.
☎ *020 7284 4631* ⊖ *Kentish Town tube.*

● THE CHARLES LAMB

Drink… in a Gallic interpretation of a London pub.

A tasteful edit of a dinky corner site in a desirable part of Islington has resulted in a quality pub with a mild French accent. It's an *entente cordiale* that works well: there are English ales, like Darkstar from Sussex, plus Breton cider; a blackboard advertises the 'Liste des vins', a sign proclaims 'Good people drink good beer', and cockerel motifs strut around. A wonderful little place.

ESSENTIAL ORDER A French aperitif is practically de rigueur – a Picon biere, which is orange bitters mixed with lager, is perfect.

16 Elia Street, Islington, N1 8DE.
☎ *020 7837 5040* 🖥 *www.thecharleslambpub.com*
⊖ *Angel tube.*

● THE WENLOCK ARMS

Drink... in a little pub that took on big business and won.

It could have been depressingly familiar. When this treasured public house came under threat of redevelopment into flats in 2010, it seemed the writing was on the wall. But regulars weren't having it: a conservation order was won from Hackney Council, and against all odds this old pub was saved and, some might say, came back stronger. It's everything you want in a London boozer – great beer, simple food, loyal locals. It's the sort of place that warms your heart just to walk past it; go inside and you'll be very glad you did. Quite possibly the best pub in London.

ESSENTIAL ORDER The huge range of ales and ciders demands your attention.
26 Wenlock Road, Hoxton, N1 7TA.
☎ *020 7608 3406*
▣ *www.wenlockarms.com*
⊖ *Old Street tube.*

- ASH GROVE MARE STREET
- CLAPTON KENNINGHALL ROAD
- FINSBURY PARK STATION
- STOKE NEWINGTON
- WHITECHAPEL LONDON HOSPITAL

● THE RAILWAY TAVERN
ALE HOUSE

Drink… in a midcentury station waiting room.
In a Georgian back street on the Islington/Hackney
borders, an old pub was given back its proper
name in 2012 along with a subtle sprucing up to
emphasise its handsome 1950s features. Now, it
brings to mind somewhere JB Priestley might settle
into for an afternoon half and the crossword while
his driver waits outside. The vintage Underground art
and carriage-compartment-brown wood transports
you to a gentler age; the superbly kept ales and craft
beers bring you pleasantly back up to date. Visit after
a dispiriting twenty-first-century commute.
ESSENTIAL ORDER A pint of something dark
and fortifying served in a proper dimpled and
handled pint glass.
2 St Jude Street, Dalston, N16 8JT.
☎ *020 0011 1195* ● *Dalston Kingsland Overground.*

● THE CLAPTON HART

Drink… in a haunted junk shop.
Taking the bric-a-brac-chic look
to a new level, this immense and
imposing pub has almost every
inch of its bare plaster walls,
floors and ceilings adorned with
bits and pieces picked up and
repurposed as decoration: de-strung
pianos turned into tables, found
furnishings, colourful bunting,
old prints and other motley items
to constantly catch the eye. This
northern part of Hackney is very
much on-the-up, and the Hart's
arty aesthetic suits it superbly.
ESSENTIAL ORDER The
dedication to local craft beers is
commendable – try one of the
many now brewed in the borough.
231 Lower Clapton Road,
Clapton, E5 8EG.
☎ *020 8985 8124*
🖥 *www.claptonhart.com*
⊖ *Clapton rail.*

● THE CARPENTER'S ARMS

Drink… in the Krays' mum's old pub.

The story goes that this comely corner site was owned by the mother of the notorious East End gangsters (their portrait's on the wall). It's a lesson in how to bring a Victorian pub up to date, bringing in a bit of modern style while preserving character. And what makes it special? On-hand owners keeping an eye on things, globetrotting beers, classy wines, a big flower display, candlesticks, chandeliers. Locals swear by it and you will too –

it's rare to find somewhere this personal so close to the relentless Brick Lane.

ESSENTIAL ORDER The twins were apparently partial to a G & T, but do you really want to be like them? The chalked-up wine list has an admirable selection of Old and New World varieties available by the glass.

73 Cheshire Street, Whitechapel, E2 6EG.
☎ *020 7739 6342*
🖳 *www.carpentersarmsfreehouse.com*
⊖ *Whitechapel tube.*

handsome front bar area, a conservatory beside the open kitchen at the back, and a side room with a wall-size map of the world where you can sit and plan your next holiday. Take some coins for the '60s jukebox.

ESSENTIAL ORDER Look out for the sparky and thirst-quenching Litovel lager on tap, imported from the Czech Republic.

50 Lichfield Road, Bow, E3 5AL.
☎ *020 8983 0130* ● *Mile End tube.*

● THE OLD FOUNTAIN

Drink... in a family-owned pub in the hipster heart of Shoreditch.

Reasons to love the Old Fountain: a wood-burning stove, cheese-and-chutney sandwiches, a blackboard chalked with a list of constantly changing ales and craft beers, a tropical fish tank, a piano, a box of farmhouse cider on the bar, family owners since 1964, a complete lack of pretension in a part of town notorious for it, old pictures of the pub's football team, Sunday roasts, a dartboard, a roof terrace, a constant welcoming thrum of chatter. Reasons not to love it: none.

ESSENTIAL ORDER You'll often spot something on tap from Beavertown Brewery – its spiritual home is just up the road in De Beauvoir Town.

3 Baldwin Street, Shoreditch, EC1V 9NU.
☎ *020 7253 2970* ▣ *www.oldfountain.co.uk*
● *Old Street tube.*

● THE LORD TREDEGAR

Drink... in Mile End's finest pub for miles around.

There aren't many of these mid-terrace Georgian pubs left in London – most of them have been turned into residences – so three cheers for the Lord T, an exceptionally tasteful remodelled old hostelry in an East End conservation area not far from Victoria Park. Anyone would be delighted to have such a pleasing place within walking distance of home – it's beautifully balanced between a

FOUNTAIN GUEST BEER

NAME	STYLE	REGION	ABV
INFANT HERCULES	BLACK IPA	MIDDLESBROUGH	5.5
KO...	PALE	HUDDERSFIELD	3.9
...ED IPA	IPA	EAST SUSSEX	6.5
...	BELGIAN FARMHOUSE	KENT	4.5
...T BITTER	LONDON	4.1
BREWERS GOLD		ESSEX	4
HOPHEAD	PALE	EAST SUSSEX	3.8
UNFILTERED	LAGER	HACKNEY	4.1 £4.20
UNFILTERED	PILSNER	NORWICH	4.0 £3.80
INDIA PALE ALE	HOPPY	NORWICH	6.0 £4.40
EXPORT INDIA	PORTER	BERMONDSEY	5.8 £5.50

● THE IVY HOUSE

Drink... in a pub that could start a revolution.

A sprawling 1930s Truman's tavern on an unprepossessing residential street near Peckham Rye... not much would suggest the Ivy House was worthy of attention, but it's a real trailblazer. Locals came together in 2012 to form a cooperative to save the building from redevelopment; in a model that could be copied all over the country, it reopened in 2013 as the first community-owned pub in Britain. It's now a genuine Nunhead hub: real ales, a kitchen serving good food, and a space for the likes of yoga, live music, theatre and storytelling.

ESSENTIAL ORDER Several London breweries are shareholders of the Ivy House. Show your support and plump for one.

40 Stuart Road, Nunhead, SE15 3BE.
☎ *020 7277 8233*
🖥 *www.ivyhousenunhead.com*
⊖ *Nunhead rail.*

● **THE GRENADIER**

Drink... in the Foot Guards' watering hole.
There's a sense of achievement that comes with finding this slightly unexpected Belgravia boozer: it's up and round the corner of a private mews running from a side street off a majestic stuccoed square. You're not going to stumble across it, that's for sure. Tourists lap up the history – it was built in 1720 to house a local army regiment – and in summer drinkers spill out on to the street among the flowers and fancy cars of Wilton Row. Out of season it's a secluded spot, with a handsome pewter bar, horsey memorabilia, a fire and loads of bay-brown wood.
ESSENTIAL ORDER Adnams Broadside was brewed to celebrate a British military victory – it's a rich, ruby-red ale.
18 Wilton Row, Belgravia, SW1X 7NR.
☎ *020 7235 3074*
⊖ *Hyde Park Corner tube.*

● PARADISE BY WAY OF KENSAL RISE

Drink... in heaven just off the Harrow Road.
Imagine a licensed version of Miss Havisham's
Satis House in Great Expectations, relocated from
Kent to Kensal Rise, and you're not far off this hugely
popular please-all pub. The shabby-chic, taxidermy-
heavy decor in the main bar is punctuated by
religious iconography; there's also a restaurant,
a club/performance space, two gardens, a library
and other nooks and crannies used for flea markets,
DJs, bands, comedy and cabaret. This means it
draws a broad a range of people, including families,
groups out for Sunday roast (the pillowy Yorkshire
puds are fantastic), boozy-brunchers, clubbers and
weekend paper readers.
ESSENTIAL ORDER The Bloody Mary is
justifiably famous, and it's not just for hangovers.
19 Kilburn Lane, Kensal Rise, W10 4AE.
☎ *020 8969 0098*
🖥 *www.theparadise.co.uk* ● *Kensal Green tube.*

● THE NAG'S HEAD

Drink… in the Duke of Westminster's local.
Two minutes' walk from the luxe-max Berkeley
hotel, past the Range Rovers and starched-shirt-
white mews flats, is this incongruous anachronism,
a knick-knack-filled retreat from the real world
with an interior the same brown as a comfy old
pair of slippers. There's a ruthlessly enforced ban

on mobiles, so you can hear the quiet retro jazz and
murmur of the contemplative pint sippers. But you'd
have to be lucky or rich to call this pub your local.
The rent is paid to the Duke of Westminster, one
of Britain's richest men: the Nag's Head is far from
aristocratic, but it's still a class act.

ESSENTIAL ORDER A dignified G & T.
53 Kinnerton Street, Belgravia, SW1X 8ED.
☎ *020 7235 1135* ⊖ *Hyde Park Corner tube.*

CRAFT BEER, ALE & CIDER

HARP • 66

JERUSALEM TAVERN • 67

CRAFT BEER CO • 68

CASK • 70

EUSTON TAP AND CIDER TAP • 70

THE BULL • 72

CAMDEN TOWN BREWERY BAR • 74

THE EARL OF ESSEX • 75

THE SOUTHAMPTON ARMS • 76

THE DOVE • 78

THE COCK TAVERN • 79

BREWDOG • 80

CRATE BREWERY • 82

THE ROYAL OAK • 84

THE CROWN & ANCHOR • 84

OLD BREWERY • 86

THE RAKE • 88

DRAFT HOUSE • 89

THE WHITE HORSE • 90

CRAFT BEER, ALE & CIDER

Porter, stout, lager, saison, fruit; craft or real, cask or keg, a bottle
or a glass… call it what you want – beer is pretty much just hops,
yeast, malt and water. And cider is more or less fermented apples.
But, of course, they're so much more than their constituent ingredients.
And they're at the heart of what pubs are all about. Before mixology,
before pork belly with kale and confit potatoes, before house wine and
alcopops and G&Ts, there was beer. And it's undergoing a full-on
renaissance in London. In 2009 there were just three breweries within
the M25 – at the last count there were more than 50, and it's growing all
the time. Similarly, artisan cider producers are springing up around the
country and sending their barrels to grateful Londoners. The bars and
pubs in this section are the ones that put real ale, craft beer and proper
cider at the forefront of everything they do. The best from local, British
and global brewers is sourced, stored and served with care, respect
and even a bit of love.

● HARP

Drink... In the beer-drinker's secret in the sightseers' heart of London.

Many pubs display beer mats above the bar like trophies of past conquests, but few can claim as many as this flower-decked free house just a couple of hundred metres from Trafalgar Square. Its enthusiasm for all things hoppy and appley wins it every award going — and what's more, it serves butcher's bangers in baguettes. A beauty.

ESSENTIAL ORDER Always resplendent on the bar is a beer from West Sussex's progressive Dark Star brewery.

47 Chandos Place, Covent Garden, WC2N 4HS.
☎ *020 7836 0291* 🖳 *www.harpcoventgarden.com*
⊖ *Charing Cross tube.*

● JERUSALEM TAVERN

Drink... in the oldest new pub in the city.

It looks ancient, and in a way it is. There was a Jerusalem Tavern in this area as long ago as the fourteenth century, but this building dates from 1719 and only became a pub in 1996. It's owned by Suffolk brewery St Peter's, and so pours little besides its own products, which is no bad thing.

Inside is a modern Clerkenwell reimagining of a seventeenth-century London inn – dark, atmospheric and kept toasty by a real fire.

ESSENTIAL ORDER Anything from St Peter's – the cream stout is especially tasty on a cold night and goes fantastically with one of the pub's sublime pork pies.
53 Britton Street, Clerkenwell, EC1M 5UQ.
☎ *020 7490 4281* 🖥 *www.stpetersbrewery.co.uk*
⊖ *Farringdon tube.*

● CRAFT BEER CO

Drink... the most adventurous selection of beer in Britain.

A fact: it's impossible to drink anything other than brilliant beer at this Leather Lane jewel. There's a commitment to small, independent British breweries, and foreign brews are imported exclusively. By the bottle are what looks like countless more, although someone has counted, and there are over 400. Such dedication means that this simply furnished place is standing-room-only most nights. If you're used to calming brown British beer, you might be pleasantly startled by the sheer daring of some of the offering – fruity Scandinavian pale ales, malty US barleywines, contemporary takes on spicy Belgian farmhouse ales.

ESSENTIAL ORDER The Craft Beer Co IPA is brewed exclusively.

82 Leather Lane, Clerkenwell, EC1N 7TR.
🖥 *www.thecraftbeerco.com*
⊖ *Farringdon tube. Branches at Brixton, Islington, Clapham, Covent Garden.*

Derbyshire's Thornbridge brews are always in high demand; the Saint Petersburg Imperial Stout takes no prisoners.
6 Charlwood Street, Pimlico, SW1V 2EE.
☎ *020 7630 7225*
💻 *www.caskpubandkitchen.com*
⊖ *Pimlico tube.*

● EUSTON TAP AND CIDER TAP

Drink... in two station bars that are worth missing your train for.
Like sentinels presiding over the planning disaster that is the modern Euston, the station's original Victorian parcel offices at the gate still stand. They've been converted into mini pubs – on the west side is the Tap, a purveyor of craft beer and British real ales; its minimal design isn't worth making a song and dance about, although stop by in summer and the crowd spreads merrily on to the pavement well into the night. A few metres opposite is its cider-prizing twin, a usually quieter sanctum for apple fanatics. It's a rural idyll in Zone 1, with a cartload of rough-hewn wood on the walls and barrels used as tables.

ESSENTIAL ORDER A powerful American IPA from Evil Twin. Over the road, Pickled Pig cider straight from the barrel.
190 Euston Road, St Pancras, NW1 2EF.
☎ *020 3137 8837* 💻 *www.eustontap.com*
⊖ *Euston tube.*

● CASK

Drink... in a craft beer pioneer.
It's a trailblazer in more ways than one – this modern and minimal place opened in 2009, just as the London craft beer revolution was in its infancy. Plus, it's on a residential street near Pimlico station, well out of the way of the city's trendy bar hotspots. Cask is another potential claimant for the title of 'biggest beer range in the city' – ignore the slightly student-union look of the place and focus instead on the wondrous selection.

● THE BULL

**Drink... in a Highgate brewpub
that stands out from the herd.**

At first glance, the Bull would appear
to be just another smart north London
gastropub, with tasteful paintwork,
a log fire and a kitchen through a big,
open hatch. But look closer, and there's
practically a field's-worth of hop
flowers hanging from the ceiling, and
behind the bar you might glimpse the
gleaming tanks and pipes of the London
Brewing Company's set-up: following
a growing trend in London, it makes
a small range of beer, sold exclusively
here. The Bull is owned by Dan Fox, who
ran the acclaimed White Horse (see
p90) for years; his thoughtful choice
of beer is the most exceptional this far
north in London.

ESSENTIAL ORDER The flagship
Beer Street is a classic best bitter, and
a great place to start.

13 North Hill, Highgate, N6 4AB.
☎ *020 8341 0510*
▣ *www.thebullhighgate.co.uk*
⊖ *Highgate tube.*

The Bull

We continuously strive to create beer that is
new, inventive and produced to the highest
quality. Our kitchen subscribes to these same
uncompromising standards. Selecting the finest,
locally sourced seasonal ingredients and working
under the belief that the right food and great
beer enhance each other exceptionally,
creating a perfect partnership.

@bull_highgate

● CAMDEN TOWN BREWERY BAR

Drink... among the tanks and pipes of Camden's party-starting brewery.

It's the sort of place you hear before you see. Head across the cobbles to the arches underneath Kentish Town West station and the growing chatter suggests something's brewing, and it's not just in the enormous steel vats of one of London's biggest beer producers. Every Thursday, Friday and Saturday Camden Town Brewery opens to drinkers – food stalls provide sustenance, DJs play, and even on winter nights the crowd sprawls from the bar to the covered and heated outdoor tables.

ESSENTIAL ORDER The rich, dry and toasty Camden Ink stout, black as the hands of a Fleet Street printer's devil.

55 Wilkin Street Mews, Kentish Town, NW5 3NN.
☎ *020 7485 1671*
🖳 *www.camdentownbrewery.com*
⊖ *Kentish Town West Overground.*

● THE EARL OF ESSEX

Drink... a short walk but a world away from Upper Street.

Far from the crowds of Islington's main (and mainstream) drinking thoroughfare, Upper Street, is a sight to cheer: on the wall of the Earl, a prominently displayed wooden board advertising the twenty choices on tap in this handsome house. Visit two days in a row and it'll look completely different – the offer changes all the time. What's more, the onsite microbrewery makes everything from highly hopped pale ales to English best bitters. A smartly outfitted garden through the back provides this blue-blood boozer with an extra dimension in the summer months.

ESSENTIAL ORDER Check the Earl's Twitter for a photo of the beer of the day.

25 Danbury Street, Islington, N1 8LE.
☎ *020 7424 5828* 🖾 *www.earlofessex.net*
⊖ *Angel tube.*

● THE SOUTHAMPTON ARMS

Drink… in London's original ale and cider house.
When it reopened in 2010, the Southampton Arms
seemed to represent something new: minimal
decor, no fancy name, no flock wallpaper or ironic
taxidermy, no kitchen… But really, it's the spirit
of the pub reborn for the twenty-first century.
Furniture is mainly restricted to penitential pews,
and the town-gas-style lamps look somewhat strict,
but a happy hubbub of customers warms things
up. The resident dog (a girl called Fred) sometimes
makes appearances, which is one reason among
many you should too.
ESSENTIAL ORDER A pint of mild next to the
coal fire (a flat cap wouldn't go amiss either).
139 Highgate Road, Kentish Town, NW5 1LE.
🖳 *www.thesouthamptonarms.co.uk*
⊖ *Gospel Oak Overground.*

● THE DOVE

Drink... in a Hackney translation of a Brussels estaminet.

With all the excitement over Britain's burgeoning craft beer scene, it's easy to forget that some nations have been brewing great ale without fuss for centuries, and never stopped. This rambling and rickety old pub has a high number of beers from the Low Countries (more than 100). Team an amber, dark, Trappist, sour or fruit beer with a bowl of moules-frites. (If you're in central London, sister pub the Dovetail is in Clerkenwell.)

ESSENTIAL ORDER The oak-aged Rodenbach Grand Cru is as complex and characterful as a vintage wine.

24 Broadway Market,
London Fields, E8 4QJ.
☎ *020 7275 7617*
🖳 *www.dovepubs.com*
⊖ *London Fields rail.*

● THE COCK TAVERN

Drink... in a back-to-basics belter of a brewpub.

An old pub reopened (in 2012) with a focus on great beer, and this one does it far better than most. For a start, there's the refurb: more a makeunder than a makeover, it highlighted the comforting features of the traditional room and left it at that. There's the brewery in the cellar, producing a range of expressive ales under the Howling Hops name. And there's the rest of the beer, which comes from independent UK brewers. Finally, when you spot the Scotch eggs and sausage rolls in their classic countertop pie cabinet, you'll be left in no doubt that this is a pretty perfect pub.

ESSENTIAL ORDER Get to grips with the mighty Howling Hops Victorian stout.

315 Mare Street, Hackney, E8 1EJ.
www.thecocktavern.co.uk
Hackney Central Overground.

● BREWDOG

Drink... with the upstart insurgents of the brewing world.

In 2006, the Aberdeenshire-based Brewdog set out to shake up the beer industry with its hop-heavy American-style creations and in-your-face marketing. This busy London bar (one of three) follows the same ethos: it's boisterous, brash and stocked with uncompromisingly flavoursome brews. The supposedly 'secret' basement (hint: it's down the stairs) serves beer cocktails and is soundtracked by suitably attitude-heavy bands.
ESSENTIAL ORDER The assertively hoppy Punk IPA is a good place to start.

51-55 Bethnal Green Road, Shoreditch, E1 6LA.
🖥 *www.brewdog.com/bars/shoreditch*
⊖ *Shoreditch High Street Overground.*
Branches at Camden Town, Shepherd's Bush.

● CRATE BREWERY

Drink... a hop, skip and jump from the Olympic Park.

Just across the canal from the site of the Games in the largely industrial Hackney Wick, this craft brewery and pizzeria opened in summer 2012 in a former workshop. It's decked out with found objects – reclaimed wood, lightshades made of old springs – and the result is one of the coolest-looking bars in London, aided by its out-of-the-way location, live jazz and DIY ideology. When it's warm, the canalside seating becomes an urban idyll, with large-scale street art, families of ducks and narrowboats pootling past. The beer is cracking, the pizzas crisp; you'll feel properly in the know when you find this place.

ESSENTIAL ORDER Crate brews are great, like the lager, bitter, pale ale and stout.

White Building, Queen's Yard, Hackney Wick, E9 5EN.
☎ *07834 275687*
🖥 *www.cratebrewery.com*
⊖ *Hackney Wick Overground.*

● THE ROYAL OAK

Drink... here when modern life overwhelms.
On a peaceful street in Borough is a timewarp: step through the doors of the Royal Oak into an era when the pub was a reassuring extension of your living room. There are leave-me-alone stools at the bar for solitary drinkers, there's a mini jumble sale on the mantelpiece, and around the carved wood central island hang what look like granny's decorative plates. Net curtains, rugs on the bare floorboards and squashy sofas complete the picture. A real one-off.

ESSENTIAL ORDER The Oak is a London tap for much-cherished Sussex brewery Harvey's. Mild, best, IPA, seasonal specials: all are tip-top.
44 Tabard Street, Borough, SE1 4JU.
☎ *020 7357 7173.* ⊖ *Borough tube.*

● THE CROWN & ANCHOR

Drink... in a beacon for Brixton beer-buffs.
One of the most profusely stocked, friendliest and all-round noteworthiest pubs in south London, and a real haven for hopheads in an otherwise dry bit of town. On the luxuriously lengthy bar is a luxurious twenty-five taps of ales, ciders and keg craft beer from the likes of Brewdog, Redwell and Windsor & Eton. The stripped-back, unadorned-brick interior is surprisingly cosy, the staff seem to know exactly what you want to drink, and on dark nights, the big Brooklyn Brewery neon on the wall is like a beacon in a stormy sea.
ESSENTIAL ORDER Brixton Brewery is just up the road – there's no finer place to sample its wares. Keep things proudly local with the amber-coloured Effra Ale.
246 Brixton Road, Stockwell, SW9 6AQ.
☎ *020 7737 0060*
▤ *www.crownandanchorbrixton.co.uk*
⊖ *Brixton tube.*

● OLD BREWERY

Drink... straight from the source.

Since its founding in 2000, Greenwich's Meantime has become a national brand, selling its beers up and down Britain. In the original brewhouse of the Old Royal Naval College, the company has opened a modern interpretation of a traditional pub with a walled suntrap of a garden; handy to know about after a panoramic stroll in Greenwich Park.

The attached restaurant holds huge copper maturation vats for the one-off brews made on site.

ESSENTIAL ORDER A limited-edition Meantime beer only available here – imperial black, say, or motueka New Zealand hop pale ale.

Pepys Building, Old Naval College,
Greenwich, SE10 9LW.
☎ *020 3327 1280*
🖥 *www.oldbrewerygreenwich.com*
⊖ *Cutty Sark DLR.*

● THE RAKE

Drink... in the greatest small bar in London bar none.

A tiny room is dotted with simple tables and chairs, a counter is cramped by a few beer taps, there's a basic heated outdoor area. Plasterboard walls are scrawled with messages from visiting brewers, all singing the praises of this no-nonsense bar; into its minimal space it crams one of London's most exciting beer selections. There are a few decent places to drink around Borough Market, and all get packed on trading days, but the Rake is worth the squeeze. (If you ever find yourself in Westfield Stratford in need of refreshment, search out sister pub Tap East, which is a grand reason to visit London's biggest shopping centre.

ESSENTIAL ORDER 'No crap on tap,' a sign proclaims – tell the staff what kind of beer you like and you'll be well rewarded.

14a Winchester Walk, Borough, SE1 9AG.
☎ *020 7407 0557* 🖥 *www.utobeer.co.uk*
⊖ *London Bridge tube.*

● DRAFT HOUSE

Drink... in a five-strong chain of bars that champions all that's brilliant about beer.
'Where the beer flows like wine,' says a sign on the wall at this 'modernised public house', and it's more than just a play on words. Along with its other locations, Draft House aims to treat the product of the grain with as much reverence as has traditionally been afforded to that of the grape. This Clapham branch should be your first choice on a street replete with bars; the others all have the knack of popping up in places that you'll be jolly pleased to find a great pub. Draft House's food, especially the aged Angus burgers, comes recommended too.
ESSENTIAL ORDER There's a 'cask of the day' sold at a very fair price, and it's often sensational.
94 Northcote Road, Clapham, SW11 6QW.
☎ *020 7924 1814* ▢ *www.drafthouse.co.uk*
⊖ *Clapham Junction Overground. Branches at City, Bermondsey, Battersea, Fitzrovia.*

● THE WHITE HORSE

Drink... in west London's beer and cider frontrunner.

Enter this airy parkside corner site, and before you notice the copper-coloured Pilsner Urquell tanks, the nut-brown armchairs, the padded pews or the almost colonial proportions of the stately room, you'll see the bar. It comes with more taps than a Bruce Forsyth routine, and features traditional British bitters, high-strength monk-brewed Belgians, and unusual examples like Italian IPA. Real beer connoisseurs turn up for festivals celebrating American, European or local brews, but the rest of us can dip into the list knowing we're in safe hands.

ESSENTIAL ORDER If you're not drinking beer here, you're not really drinking.

1-3 Parson's Green, Fulham, SW6 4UL.
☎ *020 7738 2116*
www.whitehorsesw6.com
⊖ *Parson's Green tube.*

LIQUID HISTORY

THE FRENCH HOUSE • 96

YE OLDE CHESHIRE CHEESE • 98

RULES • 99

BEAUFORT BAR AND
THE AMERICAN BAR AT THE SAVOY • 100

THE PRINCESS LOUISE • 102

AMERICAN BAR AT THE STAFFORD • 104

DUKE'S • 106

THE BLACK FRIAR • 107

YE OLDE MITRE • 108

JAMAICA WINE HOUSE • 110

THE HOLLY BUSH • 111

BOOKING OFFICE • 112

THE PROSPECT OF WHITBY • 114

THE GEORGE INN • 115

THE BAR AT THE GORING • 116

THE DOVE • 118

THE PRINCE ALFRED • 119

SATURDAY AFTERNOON

TABLE SERVICE
ONLY

SLOW

LIQUID HISTORY

The history of London's bars and pubs is the history of
London itself. From wine-sipping Romans in their tavernae through
Saxons with mead and ale to the gin-crazed Georgians and the porter-
swilling Victorians, social changes can be measured by how the city's
inhabitants drank. And nowadays, one of its unique selling points is the
history bound up in its licensed establishments. Visitors can't get enough
of the back stories: truly ancient boozers like Ye Olde Cheshire Cheese
in Fleet Street or Ye Olde Mitre in Holborn provide a glimpse into a
lost London a world away from the typical tourist zones of the West
End. And it's just as important to permanent residents too – places like
the George Inn or Rules are a connection to the centuries of Londoners
who lived here before. Some of our historical pubs have remained largely
unchanged since they were built (the Princess Louise, for example)
and with others it's not the building but the biography that deserves
a closer look – the French House was home to a whole generation
of poets, writers and actors in boho '60s Soho, and the Black Friar
is London's only extant art nouveau pub.

● THE FRENCH HOUSE

Drink... in a corner of England that is for ever a foreign land.
Soho was once London's most licentious locale, an anything-goes playground where artists, sailors, novelists, free spirits and foreigners could forget for a while they were in the capital of buttoned-up Britain. Those days are largely gone, but the French House stands as a bastion of independence and joie de vivre. During WWII, the French Resistance under Charles de Gaulle met here, inspiring its Gallic name; today, ask for a pint and you'll be offered a half only; mobiles are banned; monochrome pictures of former regulars pack the wood-panelled walls; and the two small bars resound with spirited merriment.
ESSENTIAL ORDER Find something (anything) to celebrate, drown your troubles with bubbles and get tipsy in the style of a true libertine.
49 Dean Street, Soho, W1D 5BG.
☎ *020 7437 2477*
🖳 *www.frenchhousesoho.com*
⊖ *Leicester Square tube.*

● YE OLDE CHESHIRE CHEESE

Drink... and get lost in the mists of time or in the maze of rooms.

The prefix 'Ye Olde' is open to licence, but this certainly is one extra-mature cheese. 'Rebuilt in 1667,' says the sign – after the Great Fire of London – and it looks like it's barely changed since. As such, its dim and atmospheric stone-and-wood bars and dungeon-like cellars are a huge draw for out-of-towners. It's an ancient relic they can actually sit and drink in. When a pub's been around this long it's bound to have attracted its fair share of famous Londoners; the patrons supposed to have tipped a glass here include Dickens, Yeats, Tennyson and, when the Cheese was less Olde, Dr Samuel Johnson.
ESSENTIAL ORDER In the absence of a Pepysian jug of wine, try the closest thing to the traditional smog-thick 'London particular' stout, a bottle of Taddy Porter.
145 Fleet Street, City, EC4A 2BU.
☎ *020 7353 6170* ⊖ *Chancery Lane tube.*

● RULES

Drink... in the oldest restaurant in London.
Opened in 1798, the ground-floor dining room
packs them in with its tales of notable historical
patrons and its sumptuous English fare. Upstairs,
the cocktail bar is something of a secret in
the area, and although it's a relatively more
modern addition, it shares the wonderful sense
of antiquity. The design is grandly OTT – like
an eccentric laird's Highland hunting lodge,
with leaded windows, a moulded mermaid
with stag antlers, real fur decorations come
Christmas and acres of gilt and mirrors – but the
premium spirits and expertly mixed drinks make
Rules far too good to leave to the tourists or
the traditionalists.
ESSENTIAL ORDER The Rules Cocktail is made
with gin, Dubonnet, bitters and sparkling wine.
35 Maiden Lane, Covent Garden, WC2E 7LB.
☎ *020 7836 5314* 🖳 *www.rules.co.uk*
⊖ *Covent Garden tube.*

● THE BEAUFORT BAR AND THE AMERICAN BAR AT THE SAVOY

Drink... in the world-class bars of a world-famous hotel.

Both bars in the iconic Savoy could hold a claim to being the most refined in London. Following an epic refurbishment in 2010, they reopened with two distinct but equally glamorous personalities. Past the Thames Foyer, the Beaufort is dusky, sexy, opulent and clad seductively in black and gold. The more famous American Bar, perhaps one for afternoons rather than evenings, was a birthplace of the modern cocktail and is dapper, discreet and soundtracked by a grand piano. Can there be more striking backdrops in London for the taking of drinks?

ESSENTIAL ORDER In the Beaufort, there are 25 champagnes by the glass. In the American, it has to be a classic; head barman Harry Craddock created the White Lady here in the 1920s.
Strand, WC2R 0EU. ☎ *020 7836 4343*
🖥 *www.fairmont.com/savoy-london*
⊖ *Charing Cross tube.*

● THE PRINCESS LOUISE

Drink... in a grand old London gin palace.

Once upon a time, all pubs were like this. Or, at least, pubs like this would have been less uncommon. The Princess Louise survives as a wonderful example of the late nineteenth-century 'gin palace', designed with maximum extravagance to instill in Londoners a sense that for as long as it took to drink a pint, they were lord of the manor. Take in the mirrors, the etched glass, the gold-leaf pillars, the wooden partitions, and say to yourself: they don't make them like this any more.

ESSENTIAL ORDER The pub's now under the ownership of the Samuel Smith Brewery, and its hefty and bittersweet Oatmeal Stout is the pick of the bunch.

208 High Holborn, Holborn, WC1V 7BW.
☎ *020 7405 8816*
⊖ *Holborn tube.*

● AMERICAN BAR AT THE STAFFORD

Drink... in an Ivy League clubhouse.
Most Londoners think they have no
reason to venture into the cobbled
and gaslit streets of St James's, let
alone venture further still into this
exclusive hotel. But don't let the guests
have it to themselves – The Stafford
has one of the only two American bars
left in London (they were popular in
the 1930s), and it's a unique place.
The walls and ceiling are liberally
bedecked with US memorabilia
donated by visitors over the years,
including pennants, baseball caps,
football helmets, and signed photos.
The days of gentlemen being forced to
wear a jacket and tie in the bar may
have gone, but a pleasing old-school
sensibility remains.
ESSENTIAL ORDER It has to be an
American classic – the Manhattan is
done particularly well, as you'd hope.
*The Stafford, St James's Place,
St James's, SW1A 1NJ.*
☎ *020 7493 0111* ● *Green Park tube.*

● DUKE'S

Drink... in James Bond's bar of choice.
You could order a classic cocktail. You could go
for champagne (Pol Roger Cuvée Sir Winston
Churchill seems right), or an aged calvados.
But there's one drink Duke's is famous for.
Ask for a martini, and as you sit in a Downton
Abbey armchair under historical portraits of stern
members of the landed classes, a white-jacketed
barman wheels over a trolley of chilled spirits
and exquisite glassware, and proceeds to
concoct the cocktail. It's a superb piece of
tableside theatre and one of London's quintessential
experiences, made more significant when you
learn it was Duke's that inspired author Ian Fleming
to make his 007 a Martini man. The full Bond tux
isn't necessary, but it's vital to make an effort with
your attire.
ESSENTIAL ORDER The Vesper: London gin,
Polish vodka, Lillet vermouth, bitters and orange oil.
St James's Place, St James's, SW1A 1NY.
☎ *020 7491 4840* 🖳 *www.dukeshotel.com*
⊖ *Green Park tube.*

● THE BLACK FRIAR

Drink… in an art nouveau City sanctuary.
Don't wait till you get to the end of your pint before tipping your head back in this one-of-a-kind arts-and-craft masterpiece. In friezes around the ceiling, merrie monks carouse and converse in relief, their good humour tempered somewhat by the ascetic decrees carved adjacent ('finery is foolery', for example).

ESSENTIAL ORDER Take in the arched fireplace alcove and the churchly architectural detailing and wonder at why it took a campaign from John Betjeman to save this pub from demolition in the 1960s. Then drink to its blessed continued existence.
174 Queen Victoria Street, City, EC4V 4EG.
☎ *020 7236 5474*
⊖ *Blackfriars tube.*

● YE OLDE MITRE

Drink... in a Cambridgeshire criminal's hideaway.

At one time this pub existed on land owned by the Bishop of Ely, a town in Cambridgeshire. His palace was nearby, and the story goes that felons on the run used to be able to claim refuge from City of London constabulary here. Probably best not to test that theory out, however. The Mitre was originally built in 1546, although rebuilt in 1782 and refitted inside in 1930, so its colourful history isn't immediately obvious. It's also notoriously hard to find; follow the hum of animated conversation down an alley from Hatton Garden to a cosy and characterful hideaway.

ESSENTIAL ORDER Real ales are a strong point, and the Scottish Deuchar's is usually pouring.

1 Ely Court, Holborn, EC1N 6SJ.
☎ *020 7405 4751*
🖥 *www.yeoldemitreholborn.co.uk*
⊖ *Chancery Lane tube.*

● THE JAMAICA WINE HOUSE

Drink... in an unofficial City boardroom.
On the site of this properly hidden-away City stalwart stood London's first coffee house, 'at the sign of Pasqua Rosee's Head', built in 1652 to provide a meeting place for industrious merchants. The Jamaica Wine House is now a traditional pub a world away from the big and brash chain bars that dominate the Square Mile, and it's as good for ales as it is for its titular refreshment. It's in taverns like this – reached through a maze of ancient alleyways, and with dark wood partitions – that business has been done the old-fashioned way for centuries, with a handshake, a nod and a pint.

ESSENTIAL ORDER Celebrate closing a deal (or pretend you just did) with something rich and red.

St Michael's Alley, off Cornhill, City, EC3V 9DS.
☎ *020 7929 6972* ⊖ *Bank tube.*

● THE HOLLY BUSH

Drink... at the top of a Hampstead hill.

Of all the perfectly lovely pubs in perfectly lovely Hampstead village, the Holly Bush is the most perfect. Climb through steep and winding lanes away from the post-Heath-strolling throng and you'll be rewarded by a warren of tobacco-coloured rooms and a few Fuller's beers; the Holly Bush has been an inn since 1800 and looks every year of it, in the nicest possible way (although the building itself is older).

Combine a stop-off here with a trip to the nearby seventeenth-century merchant's dwelling Fenton House. Plus, a quick fact with which to bore your drinking pals: the whole London Underground network is at its deepest point below the Holly Bush: 68.8m.
ESSENTIAL ORDER A special bottle of Fuller's Vintage. An old, old ale in an old, old pub.
22 Holly Mount, Hampstead, NW3 6SG.
☎ *020 7435 2892*
🖥 *www.hollybushhampstead.co.uk*
⊖ *Hampstead tube.*

● BOOKING OFFICE

Drink... in a Victorian cathedral of cocktails.

Housed in the former ticket office of St Pancras station and now part of the magnificent Renaissance hotel, this all-day bar and restaurant is surely one of the most impressive places to drink in London. At ground level is a sweeping marble bar, but look up and you won't fail to be awed: architect Sir George Gilbert Scott's gothic room soars with ecclesiastical arches, buttresses and leaded windows. The Victorians built pretty special pubs, but their stations were something else.

ESSENTIAL ORDER A revived classic from the 1800s: the Soyer au Champagne is made with cider brandy, cherry liqueur, vanilla ice cream and champagne.

St Pancras Renaissance, Euston Road, King's Cross, NW1 2AR.
☎ *020 7841 3566*
🖥 *www.bookingofficerestaurant.com*
⊖ *King's Cross tube.*

● THE PROSPECT OF WHITBY

Drink... in a Dickensian dockers' tavern right on the river.

The nautical history is laid on thick and unapologetically in this Wapping watering hole, reaching its peak with the modern addition of a noose on the foreshore: this was a site of piratical hangings in bygone days. 'Dating back to 1520', the pub claims – well, the flagstone floor does, at least, but even still the rest of it is sufficiently aged to give visitors a good idea of what this atmospheric area must have been like when the docks were working. Take a drink out to the terrace on a cold night and gaze out over the dark river to the wharves of Rotherhithe and the twinkling towers of Canary Wharf.

ESSENTIAL ORDER A hearty glass of grog will make the seafaring scene come to life.
57 Wapping Wall, Wapping, E1W 3SH.
☎ *020 7481 1095* ⊖ *Wapping Overground.*

● THE GEORGE INN

Drink... in London's last surviving galleried coaching inn.

This pub down a lane off Borough High Street was rebuilt in 1686, and it remains a piece of living history. It was once a stop-off for travellers making their way into the City, and has retained its balustraded galleries along the front of the building. But it's no dusty artefact. In summer, the cobbled courtyard is a magnet for workers from the surrounding and incongruously modern offices, and inside it's suitably timeworn too: the Parliament Bar, with its serving hatch, is an evocative spot.

For the full and fascinating history, see Pete Brown's excellent book *Shakespeare's Local*.

ESSENTIAL ORDER Take a drink outside and look up at the Shard – 300 years of London architecture in one glance.

75 Borough High Street, Borough, SE1 1NH.
☎ *020 7407 2056* 🖥 *www.nationaltrust.org.uk/ george-inn* ⊖ *London Bridge tube.*

● THE BAR AT THE GORING

Drink... in the Royals' favourite bar.
There are exquisite hotels aplenty in London, but few have the sense of refinement of The Goring, built in 1910 and owned by the same family since. The bar is an Edwardian haven of deep-red walls and old-school manners; drinks aren't cutting edge, although they are expertly made. Prices are high, naturally, but look at the richness of the surroundings, the courtly service and the extras like canapés in the evening and nibbles on all tables. House rules stipulate that mobiles may not be used, even when the Queen's staff have their Christmas party here. It's that sort of place.
ESSENTIAL ORDER There's half-a-million pounds-worth of wine in the cellars: it would be a shame not to try some.
The Goring, Beeston Place, Belgravia, SW1W 0JW.
☎ *020 7396 9000*
🖳 *www.thegoring.com*
⊖ *Victoria tube.*

● THE DOVE

Drink... in the world's smallest bar room.

On a sunny day, the whole of Hammersmith knows that the riverside terrace at the Dove is one of the city's most desirable. The problem with that: it's tiny, as is the rest of the centuries-old pub. So arrive early if you want to bag a prime seat overlooking a languid curve of the Thames to watch the rowers power past. Or skip the sunny season and visit in winter, when the real fire turns the flagstoned front room into one of the cosiest retreats in west London. And, keep an eye out for the hidden entrance to the tiny secret cubbyhole...

ESSENTIAL ORDER Fuller's Griffin Brewery is about half a mile upriver. On a cold day go for the London Porter, black as the midnight Thames.

19 Upper Mall, Hammersmith, W6 9TA. ☎ *020 8748 9474*
🖾 *www.dovehammersmith.co.uk*
⊖ *Hammersmith tube.*

● THE PRINCE ALFRED

Drink... in the most divisive pub in the capital.

The Victorians were a funny bunch. They built the most spectacular temples dedicated to drinking, but went out of their way to ensure that different social classes never clapped eyes on one another while patronising them. This beautifully preserved boozer not far from the canals of Little Venice has some of the most notable mid-nineteenth-century pub features left in London: 'snob' screens and partitioned snugs, originally with their own entrances to the street, shielded men from women, proles from respectable sorts, and all manner of nefarious activity from the landlord. An architectural historian's dream, and a very decent pub for the casual appreciator.

ESSENTIAL ORDER Whatever you like. No one can see you.

5a Formosa Street,
Maida Vale, W9 1EE.
☎ *020 7286 3287*
🖳 *www.theprincealfred.com*
⊖ *Warwick Avenue tube.*

WINE AND SPIRIT SPECIALISTS

TERROIRS • 124

MIZUWARI • 124

VINOTECA • 126

WHISKY BAR AT THE ATHENAEUM • 128

SHOCHU LOUNGE • 130

ARTESIAN • 131

BAR PEPITO • 132

BOISDALE • 134

BEARD TO TAIL • 136

LOUNGE BOHEMIA • 137

214 BERMONDSEY • 138

RUM KITCHEN • 138

PORTOBELLO STAR • 140

KENSINGTON WINE ROOMS • 142

WINE AND SPIRIT SPECIALISTS

Some occasions call for something other than a pint of beer.
A refreshing gin and tonic on a hot summer evening, a warming
brandy on a frosty night, a glass of something white and vivacious
(or red and fruity), a sweet, salty, smoky or peaty malt whisky…
All the bars in this chapter are noted for their commitment to the
grape and the grain, whether it's the hundreds of varieties of Scotch
in Boisdale, the extraordinary natural wines in Terroirs, or the shrine
to high-class rum that is Artesian. And it's a good time to be a
specialist in spirits. Following a fallow few decades, there are several
enthusiastic producers making small-batch gin in London again,
from Highgate's Sacred to the gingery, citrussy Little Bird;
around the city, discerning drinkers are recognising the merits
of mezcal, sipping tequilas, barrel-aged rums and sherries.
More unconventional spirits are entering the mainstream too –
pisco, shochu, soju, Japanese whisky. And London is a wine-drinker's
paradise: the city's auctioneers break records with the world's
most expensive bottles of wine, but its bars are fortunately
more egalitarian.

average bottle of supermarket plonk – emphatic, often wildly unfettered flavours ('farmy' is one complimentary description used). You don't have to eat here, but the small plates, charcuterie and cheese are excellent partners to the wines.

ESSENTIAL ORDER The earthy, dark-fruited Vino di Anna 'Jeudi 15' is typical of the natural winemaking technique.

5 William IV Street, Covent Garden, WC2N 4DW. ☎ *020 7036 0660* ⌨ *www.terroirswinebar.com* ⊖ *Charing Cross tube.*

● MIZUWARI

Drink... in a Shinjuku whisky joint.
Sake might be seen as the national drink of Japan, but the Japanese themselves are officially mad for whisky. The founders of the country's eight distilleries learned their art in Scotland, and their products are every bit as subtle and involving as Scotch. This dark and intriguing basement bar has one of the largest ranges in London, and whether you have a single malt served over a chunk of hand-cracked ice, with water (mizuwari) or in a cocktail, this bar is a great introduction to the drink.

ESSENTIAL ORDER If you're a newcomer to Japanese whisky, let the knowledgeable staff be your guide.

16 Old Compton Street, Soho, W1D 4TL. ☎ *020 7287 9111* ⌨ *www.bincho.co.uk/whisky-joint* ⊖ *Tottenham Court Road tube.*

● TERROIRS

Drink... a delicious glass of white, red, rosé or orange.
Yes, orange wine does exist (it's basically white grapes macerated in the red wine style), and it's a style all of its own. Terroirs is one of the best places in London to try natural and biodynamic wines, which are made by fanatical small-scale viticulturalists, in tune with the seasons, unfiltered, unsulphured and using strict organic methods. The results are very unlike your

● VINOTECA

Drink... in a democratic wine bar that could make oenophiles of us all.

There are few wine bars in London that put so much thought and care into their offering, with a list running to hundreds of bottles, all chosen from exciting producers. It's also affordable – there are 25 by the glass (kept fresh in an Enomatic preservation machine), and prices start at under £4. Excellent cheese and charcuterie keeps the peckish satisfied, but Vinoteca is also a splendid restaurant in its own right. **ESSENTIAL ORDER** For a discreet little treat, there's prosecco on tap. Hard to say no to that.

53 Beak Street, Soho, W1F 9SH.
☎ *020 3544 7411*
🖾 *www.vinoteca.co.uk*
⊖ *Piccadilly Circus tube.*
Branches at Farringdon, Chiswick, Marylebone.

● WHISKY BAR AT THE ATHENAEUM

Drink... a different whisky for every day of the year...

...almost. There are 364 here, to be precise, so just pick your day off and get started. Less regular visitors to this suave Mayfair hotel bar may find the choice on one of the biggest lists in London daunting, but help is at hand, as the Athenaeum employs a whisky sommelier. Highlights are almost too plentiful to mention; the hotel works with distilleries and independent bottlers to source one-off and hard-to-find expressions. Connoisseurs should book a whisky and cheese pairing session, where they'll learn among other things that the ideal match for Balvenie Doublewood 12-year-old is a blue cheese from Inverness-shire.

ESSENTIAL ORDER Splash out on a Highland Park 25-year-old, smoky and sweet like a burning beehive.

116 Piccadilly, Mayfair, W1J 7BJ.
☎ *020 7499 3464*
🖥 *www.athenaeumhotel.com*
⊖ *Green Park tube.*

● SHOCHU LOUNGE

Drink... Japan's favourite spirit.

Everyone's heard of sake, and it's well known that the Japanese venerate whisky too, but actually the country's most-supped alcoholic drink after beer is shochu, still fairly rare in the West. It's distilled from various bases including grains, sweet potatoes and vegetables, each giving it a different character, plus fruits and herbs are used as infusions too. In this sleek, metropolitan underground bar it's served neat over hand-carved blocks of ice or shaken into sophisticated cocktails with Eastern additions like yuzu, green tea and rosewater.

ESSENTIAL ORDER A plum ume shu – straight – to acquaint yourself with this delicate spirit.

37 Charlotte Street, Fitzrovia, W1T 1RR.

☎ *020 7580 6464*

🖳 *www.shochulounge.com*

⊖ *Goodge Street tube.*

● ARTESIAN

Drink... at a five-star bar that almost didn't exist.

It's hard to believe when you survey the monumental edifice of the grand Langham hotel, or marvel at the marble and towering columns in its sumptuous bar, but over its 150-year history it was damaged by aerial bombing, commandeered by the BBC and survived a 1980 proposal to demolish. It now serves as the ideal high-class haven for footsore shoppers from Oxford Street. The cocktails are rightly lauded (although some are presented with what is more tableside pantomime than theatre), but rum is a speciality, and the lavish and grandiose room is a great place for an afternoon glass of wine too.

ESSENTIAL ORDER One of the many superior sipping rums, like Brugal Extra Viego from the Dominican Republic: spicy, nutty and treacly as a Christmas cake.

1C Portland Place, Marylebone, W1B 1JA.

☎ *020 7636 1000*

▦ *www.artesian-bar.co.uk*

⊖ *Oxford Circus tube.*

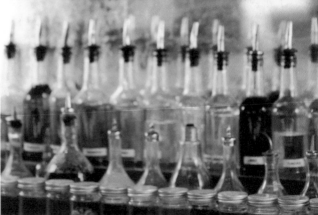

● BAR PEPITO

Drink... in an Andalusian bodega.

With around twenty sherries to try by the glass, Bar Pepito should be your first stop in an exploration of the layers and subtleties of this underappreciated but resurgent fortified wine. It fits right into its cavern-like ex-warehouse space in a regenerated bit of King's Cross, with Spanish knick-knacks on the walls completing an authentic Iberian look. Staff really know their stuff, advising on which sherries best complement the fancied-up tapas on offer (a 'reconstructed' tortilla, for example).

ESSENTIAL ORDER A desert-dry manzanilla La Gitano or a honeyed matusalem.

Varnishers Yard, King's Cross, N1 9FD.

☎ *020 7841 7331*

▭ *www.barpepito.co.uk*

⊖ *King's Cross tube.*

● BOISDALE

Drink… in a Highland castle on the Isle of Dogs.

It's an understatement to say there's whisky galore at this eastern branch of the three-strong Boisdale group. The vast space is a feast of Caledoniana, with yards of tartan, stuffed game trophies and stately leather armchairs, and one of London's few cigar terraces. Perch at the counter in front of the magnificent 12-metre display of bottles and allow the whisky-encyclopedia of a barman to talk you through your choices. There's something from just about every Scottish distillery, silent and operational, as well as rare and limited-edition expressions. It gets pricey – over £600 for a Black Bowmore 1964 Sherry Cask – but there's something for all pockets as well as palates.

ESSENTIAL ORDER An exclusive Boisdale bottling – Longmorn or Linkwood from Speyside, Teaninich or Clynelish from the Highlands.
Cabot Place, Canary Wharf, E14 4QT.
☎ *020 7715 5818*
🖾 *www.boisdale.co.uk*
⊖ *Canary Wharf tube. Branches at Belgravia and Bishopsgate.*

● BEARD TO TAIL

Drink... in an East End Deep South barbecue pit.
The roasted, smoked and grilled meats on the menu at this US-meets-GB bar and restaurant are mouthwatering, but if it's a drink you're hankering after, you won't be disappointed. The cocktails are great, especially the whiskey-based creations (the Rocket Fuel is made with rye, smoked porter reduction, lemon and whiskey-barrel bitters), but most impressive is the range of ryes, bourbons and Tennessee whiskeys. Many are old and rare, like the FEW unaged White Dog, or Willett's bourbon: sweet, buttery and nutty like a Kentucky Derby pie.

ESSENTIAL ORDER Put some South in your mouth with the house Julep, made with bourbon, mint, and peach and cinnamon jam.
77 Curtain Road, Shoreditch, EC2A 3BS.
☎ *020 7729 2966* ✉ *www.beardtotail.co.uk*
⊖ *Shoreditch High Street Overground.*

● LOUNGE BOHEMIA

Drink... in a Cold War Eastern Bloc jazz bunker.
You could walk past the anonymous doorway of
this clandestine basement without ever knowing
it was here, and every night thousands of beered-
up City/Shoreditch types do. The website doesn't
give much away either. But here's the intelligence:
you absolutely must book and you won't get in
wearing a suit. When you've passed those tests,
you'll find a diminutive cocktail bar dressed simply
in midcentury furniture which does a great line in
everything Czech – eaux de vie, homemade infused
vodkas, Regent Bohemian lager, borovicka juniper
brandy, Becherovka bitters... Don't overlook the
avant-garde cocktails, though, which are incredible.
ESSENTIAL ORDER The Old Castro – cigar-
infused rum, vanilla candy floss, orange bitters and
a large measure of bar performance.
1e Great Eastern Street, Shoreditch, EC2A 3EJ.
☎ *07720 707000* 🖥 *www.loungebohemia.com*
⊖ *Shoreditch High Street Overground.*

● 214 BERMONDSEY

Drink... the true spirit of London.

Gin is the definitive London drink. It's gone from the cheap and cheerless 'mother's ruin' of Hogarth's day to something endlessly varied and sophisticated. And this dusky basement bar near Borough has a huge stock of the stuff, including every local variety, like Highgate's Sacred, Bermondsey's Jensen and Hammersmith's Sipsmith, as well as bottles from all over the world. Bermondsey 214 might not be much of a looker, but sit at the bar and admire the range.

The dedication to gin is so complete that bartenders make their own tonic here: it's subtle and natural to let the flavours of the spirit speak out.

ESSENTIAL ORDER Indecisive? Take a 'flight' – three themed gins with some of that tonic.

214 Bermondsey Street, Bermondsey, SE1 3TQ.
☎ *020 7403 6875* 🖳 *www.214-bermondsey.co.uk*
⊖ *Borough tube.*

● RUM KITCHEN

Drink... in a West Indian beach shack for the west London set.

Despite the driftwood panelling, Rum Kitchen could hardly be called rustic – Prince Harry is among the sort of castaways who wash up here. But it's a lively and always rocking joint, a place to treat rum with reverence or just knock it back in the fantastic cocktails. The dark basement below the restaurant resonates to the sound of reggae and other island vibes, and the barmen know everything there is to know about the spirit of the Caribbean.

ESSENTIAL ORDER Daquiri, Zombie or punch: they're all made with aplomb, although there's a bounty-worth of rums to be sipped and savoured.

6 All Saints Road, Notting Hill, W11 1HH.
☎ *020 7920 6479* 🖳 *www.therumkitchen.com*
⊖ *Ladbroke Grove tube. Branch at Soho.*

● PORTOBELLO STAR

Drink... in London's only gin museum.

Is there anyone more passionate about the history, distilling and drinking possibilities of gin than the founders of the Star? On the ground floor is a good-times Notting Hill bar with an enormous range of gins, vintage spirits and single-botanical infusions. Upstairs is the Ginstitute – a space dedicated to educating the curious imbiber about the wondrous spirit itself. Book a session, which can be as serious or as fun as you like, and you'll leave with your own bespoke bottle. A ginspirational place.

ESSENTIAL ORDER The house gin martini, made with Portobello Road gin, Lillet Blanc vermouth, bitters and a twist of grapefruit.

171 Portobello Road,
Notting Hill, W11 2DY.
☎ *020 7229 8016*
🖳 *www.portobellostarbar.co.uk*
⊖ *Ladbroke Grove tube.*

● KENSINGTON WINE ROOMS

Drink... help-yourself tasters of wines for every inclination.

There are few places in London that take wine so seriously or strive to make drinking it an experience for all to enjoy as this chic bar among the posh antique shops of Kensington Church Street. A swish Enomatic machine keeps 40 bottles fresh and available by the glass, plus there's a neat option to load a card with credit and get sampling. Experts are on hand to dispense advice.

ESSENTIAL ORDER Wines start at around £4 a glass – dive in and start exploring.

127 Kensington Church Street, Kensington, W8 7LP.
☎ *020 7727 8142*
▥ *www.greatwinesbytheglass.com*
⊖ *Notting Hill Gate tube.*
Branch at Fulham.

WITH A TWIST

MR FOGG'S • 148

APE & BIRD • 150

THE AULD SHILLELAGH • 151

THE DUKE OF CAMBRIDGE • 152

THE FALTERING FULLBACK • 153

THE PALM TREE • 154

THE BOOK CLUB • 155

THE PRIDE OF SPITALFIELDS • 156

WELL & BUCKET • 157

MAYOR OF SCAREDY CAT TOWN • 158

AQUA SHARD • 160

FRANK'S CAFE • 162

THE SHIP • 163

LITTLE BAR • 164

THE MAYFLOWER • 165

CABLE CAFE • 166

THE HARWOOD ARMS • 168

TRAILER HAPPINESS • 170

WITH A TWIST

In a city with so many bars and pubs, there are bound to be
a few that break the mould. Those which diverge from the usual
'room in which to drink' model. There are loads of eccentric,
idiosyncratic and downright unusual drinking establishments
in London. But just because a bar has a silly name, or a password
is required to get in, or it's at the top of a tall building, doesn't mean
it's actually worth leaving the house for. The places in this chapter,
however, all have something that set them apart from the masses,
and they're more than deserving of your custom. Some are local pubs,
some are high-end cocktail bars, but all are uncategorisable.
They're for special occasions, for celebrations, for perking up
a mundane Monday night, for those times when you need more
than just a pub quiz to keep you entertained.

● MR FOGG'S

Drink... in the souvenir-stuffed home of a Victorian explorer.

On paper, it sounds a bit silly – a Phileas Fogg-themed room displaying all manner of artefacts from the fictional gentleman's travels: a hot-air balloon, flags, penny farthings, animal trophies... But underneath this fastidiously observed theme, there's a very good bar. Service is courteous and eager-to-please, the leather seats are generously plush, and the cocktails are expertly made.

ESSENTIAL ORDER

The bracing East India – a mixture of European and tropical constituents – seems apt.

15 Bruton Lane, Mayfair, W1J 6JD.

☎ *020 7299 1200*

🖥 *www.mr-foggs.com*

⊖ *Green Park tube.*

● APE & BIRD

**Drink... in a reinvented gastropub with
a secret in its cellar.**

Some might argue that the pub doesn't need
updating, but if it has to be done, this is the blueprint.
The folk behind a small but hugely hip group of bar/
restaurants (Polpo, Spuntino and others) opened this
prominent place on Shaftesbury Avenue in late 2013
and labelled it a 'public house', but it doesn't look
much like your average Dog & Duck. On the ground
floor is a casual restaurant and a separate (almost)
traditional drinking space, but the real appeal
comes with the downstairs 'dive bar', a seductively
lit and secretive spot with simple cocktails and
high-backed booths for groups. Among the theatres,
chains, rip-offs and endless crowds of the West End,
this is a highly civilised hideaway.

ESSENTIAL ORDER A herbaceous and vivacious
southern European digestif – the Aperol Spritz goes
down easy.

142 Shaftesbury Avenue, Covent Garden, WC2H 8HJ.
☎ *020 7836 3119* 🖥 *www.apeandbird.com*
⊖ *Leicester Square tube.*

● THE AULD SHILLELAGH

Drink... in Ireland, in Hackney.

The staff are all Irish, the customers all seem to be Irish, the pennants and pictures on the walls of this narrow Stoke Newington boozer are all Irish. At weekends a live band fiddles and strums away in the corner. There's not much other than Guinness to drink, although enough of it must be sunk here to fill Galway Bay. Among London's many Irish-ish pubs, the Auld Shillelagh stands out as a genuinely foot-tapping, hand-clapping, glass-clinking Emerald Isle gem. It's enough to make you yearn for the old country, even if your experience starts and ends with a 0735 Ryanair flight to Dublin.

ESSENTIAL ORDER What else but the black stuff, poured perfectly every time.

105 Stoke Newington Church Street,
Stoke Newington, N16 0UD.
☎ *020 7249 5951*
⊖ *Stoke Newington rail.*

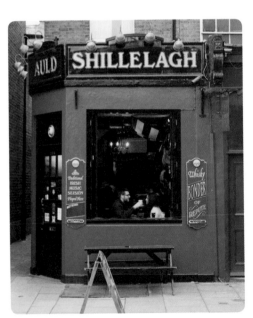

● THE DUKE OF CAMBRIDGE

Drink... in Britain's only organic pub.

A true groundbreaker when it opened in 1998, this spacious and rustic Islington pub is still the only one in Britain to ensure everything served is organic. Food is to the fore, and it's very good, but the environmental-minded drinker will find plenty to keep them satisfied. It's 100 percent certified: ales from around Britain, some of them brewed especially for the bar, organic and biodynamic wines from England and beyond, and spirits including Highgrove gin and Bruichladdich malt whisky.

ESSENTIAL ORDER It's all organic, so it's all sort-of good for you. Take your pick!

30 Peter's Street, Islington, N1 8JT.
☎ *020 7359 3066*
🖥 *www.sloeberry.co.uk*
⊖ *Angel tube.*

● THE FALTERING FULLBACK

Drink... in a vertical garden that grows up and up.
This slightly suburban oddity is like three pubs in one. There's a casual front bar hung with all sorts of junk-shop esoterica, and a sports-friendly back room with big screens showing all the football and rugby, but the real draw is the garden. Its footprint is small but it takes to the skies – stacked up are four decked floors, some covered, some open, festooned with flowers, plants and trinkets, all offering numerous opportunities to sit in a vertical horticultural paradise.
ESSENTIAL ORDER A cold Vedett lager amid the greenery is hard to beat come summer.
19 Perth Road, Stroud Green, N4 3HB.
☎ *020 7272 5834*
🖥 *www.thefullback.co.uk*
⊖ *Finsbury Park tube.*

● THE PALM TREE

Drink... in the imagined East End of jellied eels and gentlemen gangsters.
The Palm Tree stands on its own. Literally, as it's the sole survivor of a war-bombed terrace, meaning it cuts a lonely figure in Mile End Park; and figuratively too – 'distinctive' doesn't even begin to cover it. Gold-embossed flock wallpaper, red velvet drapes, slightly seedy orange lighting, an ancient cash register, old cockneys communing at the bar and a jazz band in the corner... It's outlived every design fad from the last thirty years and remains a true one-of-a-kind. In the summer, drinkers make the most of the green canalside location. Be warned, though: the Palm Tree famously doesn't serve tap water, meaning you'll have to search for another oasis if you're dying of thirst.
ESSENTIAL ORDER The attraction here isn't what you're drinking, it's where you're drinking it. But there are usually a couple of uncomplicated real ales on.
127 Grove Road, Mile End, E3 5BH.
☎ *020 8980 2918*
⊖ *Mile End tube.*

● **THE BOOK CLUB**

Drink... in a twenty-first-century social club.
Thankfully a lot more exciting than its name suggests, the Book Club provides all manner of enlightening distraction for Shoreditch in its imaginatively fitted-out space. Both the breakfast-to-late-night food and the party-time drinks are enough to keep anyone off the streets, but check out the extracurricular activities: a packed events timetable includes DJs and bands, craft classes, yoga, quizzes, jumble sales, film nights, talks, life drawing... And a permanent ping pong table even allows for a bit of exercise. There's no bar in London that puts so much effort into keeping its patrons entertained.
ESSENTIAL ORDER Take a group of pals and get stuck in to the jugs of cocktails to share.
100 Leonard Street, Shoreditch, EC2A 4RH.
☎ *020 7684 8618*
🖥 *www.wearetbc.com*
⊖ *Old Street tube.*

● THE PRIDE OF SPITALFIELDS

Drink... in the coolest uncool pub in London.
Most of the bars around Brick Lane have
followed fashion to cater for the hordes of hipsters
who flock to this famous old street nightly –
but not the Pride. With its net curtains, wood-
burning stove, patterned carpet and blood-red
walls, it's a glimpse into an East End largely lost –
but as well as that, it's a friendly, cosy and quirky
place to escape the real world. Youngsters on
nights out rub shoulders with seasoned locals
and elderly fixtures who look like they never
leave the place, while the pub cat surveys it all
disinterestedly.

ESSENTIAL ORDER Something by London
microbrewery Truman's – it was made for
more than 300 years at the Black Eagle Brewery
nearby in Brick Lane.
3 Heneage Street, Whitechapel, E1 5LJ.
☎ *020 7247 8933*
⊖ *Aldgate East tube.*

● WELL & BUCKET

Drink... in a Victorian pub that came back from the dead.

By 2012, the Well & Bucket was a sad sight: the premises had been occupied by a leather goods wholesaler then closed completely. But in 2013 it reopened for its intended purpose, and revealed a real stunner beneath the years of neglect: original tiles, now restored with a modern macabre twist. It's now busy and buzzing, and craft beer is its speciality, with 18 on draft; in the dark and secretive vaults of the pub's old cellar is the 5CC cocktail club, which would be worthy of an entry in this book on its own.

ESSENTIAL ORDER A Kernel London porter with oysters upstairs; a short and punchy cocktail downstairs.

143 Bethnal Green Road, Bethnal Green, E2 7DG.
☎ *020 3664 6454*
🖥 *www.wellandbucket.com*
⊖ *Shoreditch High Street Overground.*

● MAYOR OF SCAREDY CAT TOWN

Drink... in a fridge.

Well, to be more accurate, behind a fridge. The chiller in question is a retro American model in Spitalfields diner the Breakfast Club: tell a staff member you're here to see the mayor, and a secret door leads down to what might be the daftest-named bar in London – and maybe the most frolicsome too. In an era of po-faced Prohibition pretenders, it's great to see somewhere take the 'speakeasy' theme with far more than the recommended pinch of salt. The 'house rules' includes an insistence you leave by a different exit to maintain the secrecy.

ESSENTIAL ORDER The classic cocktails are all straightforward but splendid.

12 Artillery Lane, Spitalfields, E1 7LS.

☎ 020 7078 9639

🖃 www.themayorofscaredycattown.com

⊖ Liverpool Street tube.

● AQUA SHARD

Drink... in some views with your booze.
Few bars match up in height to Aqua Shard, sandwiched halfway up the tallest and pointiest building in the EU. At 114 metres above the scurrying pedestrians and toy-sized trains of London Bridge, Aqua's one of the most altitudinous bars in London, and it's the spectacular floor-to-ceiling vista that make it worth the trip up in the lift. All 32 boroughs (plus the City) spread out around in a gloriously elaborate panoply of streets, tower blocks, parks, churches, railway lines and countless iconic structures to point out. Every seat comes with something different and endlessly fascinating to look at — which makes Aqua an ideal spot if you're worried conversation might dry up...

ESSENTIAL ORDER The inventive tea-based cocktails are a cut above — try Heaven On Earth, with aged rum, sherry, tangerine and pistachio maple syrup.
Level 31, The Shard, 31 St Thomas Street, Borough, SE1 9RY.
☎ *020 3011 1256*
🖥 *www.aquashard.co.uk*
⊖ *Borough tube.*

● FRANK'S CAFÉ

Drink... in an art-filled concrete car park with a view.

Ten floors up in a deserted car park in Peckham... It doesn't sound like the setting for one of London's most consistently cool bars, but scale the heights and you'll be rewarded with not only large-scale new sculpture works on the way up, but an arresting panorama of the city from an unusual aspect when you arrive at the top. The downside, so to speak: it's only operational over the summer months and is open to the elements – dress accordingly.

ESSENTIAL ORDER Simple cocktails, simple food – a Negroni, ox-heart skewers.

Tenth floor, Peckham Multistorey Car Park, 95a Rye Lane, Peckham, SE15 4ST.

www.frankscafe.org.uk

Peckham Rye Overground.

● THE SHIP

Drink... in the finest Thames-side pub till Oxford.
The Ship has been serving thirsty Wandsworth workers since it opened as a riverside inn in 1786, but the eighteenth-century waterman might not recognise it nowadays, especially in summer. Despite the unpromising location next to a cement-landing wharf, it's massively popular – the cosy and quiet public bar has been augmented with a conservatory, restaurant and impressive beer garden complete with its own bar. There can't be many pubs with the space to pack in so many drinkers and puts them all in solid sight of the upstream Thames.

ESSENTIAL ORDER Sambrook's Wandle – a refreshing south London ale that goes hand-in-hand with sunshine and water.

41 Jews Row, Wandsworth, SW18 1TB.
☎ *020 8870 9667* 🖳 *www.theship.co.uk*
⊖ *Wandsworth Town rail.*

● LITTLE BAR

Drink… in a less-than-large local you'll long to live near.

By the time you leave this diminutive Tooting drinkery you'll probably want to open your own little bar. How hard can it be, you'll think – but Little Bar makes it look easy. Everything seems to suit the size – the small list of cocktails, spirits, beers, ciders and wines is clearly chosen with great consideration, and there are platefuls of cheese and charcuterie. Grab one of the stools and before long you'll probably get to know the chatty staff too.

ESSENTIAL ORDER Negronis are a speciality: have an 'Unusual' one with Hendrick's gin.

145 Mitcham Road, Tooting, SW17 9PE.
☎ *020 8672 7317*
⊖ *Tooting Broadway tube.*

● THE MAYFLOWER

Drink... with your feet in the Thames.
On a peaceful stretch of the river,
in tucked-away Rotherhithe, is this
picturesque and historic little pub. It
would be special even if it was solidly
on dry land, but it backs right on to the
Thames: stand on the wooden deck
projecting over the water and watch
the wash slap against the pillars below.
It's particularly pleasing at night, when
the towers of the City sparkle in the
distance. Inside is equally attractive
– there's a fire, wooden pews, framed
antique manuscripts and various
pertinent mottos inscribed on the walls.
An enchanting place.
ESSENTIAL ORDER Take a mulled
wine and a blanket (both provided!)
outside on a dark and chilly evening
and watch the riverboats speed by.
*117 Rotherhithe Street, Rotherhithe,
SE16 4NF.*
☎ *020 7237 4088*
🖥 *www.themayflowerrotherhithe.com*
⊖ *Rotherhithe Overground.*

● **CABLE CAFE**

Drink... in a perfect noir of a bar.
At night, this singular little spot
is one of the most atmospheric
hideaways in London. Beside a neon
manual coffee machine and below
old railway station lamps, couples
chat in hushed tones and lone
readers repose like Left Bank poets
against a soundtrack of mellifluent
jazz. The tobacco-brown wood walls
are dotted with various vintage
bits and pieces, bands sometimes
play in a corner, there's no written
menu, mobile phones somehow
seem inappropriate. A place to lose
yourself for a while.
ESSENTIAL ORDER Something
strong, neat and Continental –
how about a Campari on ice (or even
a double espresso)?
8 Brixton Road, Kennington,
SW9 6BU.
☎ *020 8617 9629*
☐ *Oval tube.*

● THE HARWOOD ARMS

Drink... among the rolling fields and country lanes of Fulham.
This pretty and elegantly scuffed place pushes the boundaries of what can be called a pub. One can indeed sit and just order a drink, but the set tables and attentive waiters leave no doubt that this is a gastropub. And not just any gastropub: Fulhamites flock here for the Michelin-starred food, much of which is game shot in the Home Counties (see the monochrome portraits on the walls of hunting parties and be left in no doubt where your plateful came from). Drinkers can tuck into bar snacks – roe deer and walnut terrine, say. A pack of peanuts will never again suffice.

ESSENTIAL ORDER The elegant wines by the glass go down rather nicely with a soft-yolked venison Scotch egg.

Walham Grove, Fulham, SW6 1QP.
☎ *020 7386 1847*
🖥 *www.harwoodarms.com*
⊖ *West Brompton tube.*

● TRAILER HAPPINESS

Drink... in a '70s Hawaiian beach lounge.

Three wines, three beers, but barrel-loads of rum – this Notting Hill basement bar is all about totally tropical cocktails to be drank with tongue in cheek (one contains Ribena). It's on the tiki side of tacky, with groovy patterned wallpaper, Eero Aarnio-style armchairs and wallfuls of JH Lynch 'Tina' prints. A riot.

ESSENTIAL ORDER That old Polynesian favourite, the Zombie, comes with nine rums, spiced syrup, cherry, absinthe and lime.
177 Portobello Road, Notting Hill, W11 2DY.
☎ *020 7313 4644*
🖥 *www.trailerhappiness.com*
⊖ *Ladbroke Grove tube.*

TICK INDEX

☐ 69 Colebrooke Row p26

☐ American Bar at the Stafford p104

☐ Ape & Bird p150

☐ Aqua Shard p160

☐ Artesian p131

☐ The Auld Shillelagh p151

☐ Bar Américain p22

☐ The Bar at the Goring p116

☐ Bar Pepito p132

☐ Beard to Tail p136

☐ The Beaufort Bar and the American Bar at the Savoy p101

☐ 214 Bermondsey p138

☐ The Black Friar p107

☐ The Blue Bar p32

☐ Boisdale p134

☐ The Book Club p155

☐ Booking Office p112

☐ Brewdog p80

☐ The Bull p72

☐ Cable Cafe p166

☐ Callooh Callay p34

☐ Camden Town Brewery Bar p74

☐ The Carpenter's Arms p52

☐ Cask p70

☐ The Charles Lamb p45

☐ The Clapton Hart p50

☐ Coburg Bar at the Connaught p20

☐ The Cock Tavern p79

☐ Cocktail Lounge at the Zetter Townhouse p16

☐ Craft Beer Co p69

☐ Crate Brewery p82

☐ The Crown & Anchor p84

☐ The Dove, W6 p118

☐ The Dove, E8 p78

☐ Draft House p89

☐ The Duke of Cambridge p152

☐ Duke's p106

☐ The Earl of Essex p75

☐ Euston Tap and Cider Tap p70

☐ Experimental Cocktail Club p14

☐ The Faltering Fullback p153

☐ Frank's Café p162

☐ The French House p96

☐ The George Inn p115

☐ Grain Store p28

☐ The Grenadier p57

☐ Happiness Forgets p28

☐ Harp p66

☐ The Harwood Arms p168

☐ Hawksmoor p36

☐ The Holly Bush   p111
☐ The Island Queen   p42
☐ The Ivy House   p56
☐ Jamaica Wine House   p110
☐ Jerusalem Tavern   p67
☐ Kensington Wine Rooms   p142
☐ Little Bar   p164
☐ London Cocktail Club   p14
☐ The Lord Tredegar   p54
☐ Lounge Bohemia   p137
☐ Mark's Bar   p24
☐ The Mayflower   p165
☐ Mayor of Scaredy Cat Town   p158
☐ Milk & Honey   p18
☐ Mizuwari   p124
☐ Mr Fogg's   p148
☐ The Nag's Head   p60
☐ Nightjar   p30
☐ Old Brewery   p86
☐ The Old Fountain   p54
☐ Oskar's Bar   p18
☐ The Palm Tree   p154
☐ Paradise by Way of Kensal Rise   p58
☐ The Pineapple   p44
☐ Portobello Star   p140
☐ The Pride of Spitalfields   p156

☐ The Prince Alfred   p119
☐ The Princess Louise   p102
☐ The Prospect of Whitby   p114
☐ Punch Room   p21
☐ The Queen's Head   p42
☐ The Railway Tavern Ale House   p49
☐ The Rake   p88
☐ The Royal Oak   p84
☐ Rules   p99
☐ Rum Kitchen   p138
☐ The Ship   p163
☐ Shochu Lounge   p130
☐ The Southampton Arms   p77
☐ Terroirs   p124
☐ Trailer Happiness   p170
☐ Vinoteca   p126
☐ Well & Bucket   p157
☐ The Wenlock Arms   p46
☐ Whisky Bar at the Athenaeum   p128
☐ The White Horse   p90
☐ White Lyan   p34
☐ Worship Street Whistling Shop   p35
☐ Ye Olde Cheshire Cheese   p98
☐ Ye Olde Mitre   p108

Frances Lincoln Limited
74–77 White Lion Street
London N1 9PF
www.franceslincoln.com

Drink London
Copyright © Frances Lincoln 2014
Text copyright © Euan Ferguson 2014
Photographs copyright © Kim Lightbody 2014
Except the following: p.4 The Artesian © Bernard Zieja;
p.20 Coburg bar © Damian Russell; p.32–33 © The Blue Bar;
p.106 © Duke's Bar; p.162 Frank's Café © Richard Bryant
Maps copyright © Red Sky Studio 2014

A catalogue record for this book is available
from the British Library.

ISBN 978-0-7112-3581-6
Printed and bound in China

9 8 7 6 5 4 3